To ....

From the fullness of his grace we have all received
one blessing after another.

JOHN 1:16

From ....

Faith
HOPE
LOVE

by Sheila Walsh

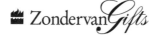

Zondervan*Gifts*

Senior Editor: Gwen Ellis
Project Editor: Sarah Hupp
Design: Big Cat Marketing Communications

Printed in the United States of America

98 99 00/WP/ 3 2 1

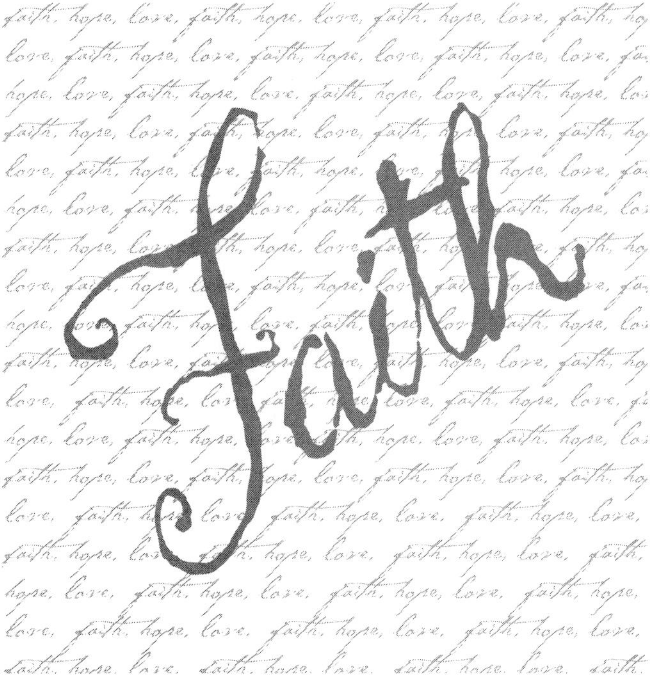
faith
faith, hope, love,

F A I T H

Without faith it is impossible to please God,
because anyone who comes to him must believe that he exists
and that he rewards those who earnestly seek him.

HEBREWS 11:6

6

F A I T H

I want to know the whole game plan.

I want to know what roads I will be on, where they will take me,

how long it will take, and when it will all happen.

But as a follower of Christ, all I am called to do

is to take the next step.

F A I T H

One of the greatest adventures of my life is to face the truth
about myself, to face my fears, to let everything go and to
trust God in the darkness. Whatever comes into my life,
whether it is what I would choose or not, can be used
by the Lord to mold my life if I will rest in him.

F A I T H

Sometimes I think we misinterpret faith.

I thought if I just *believed* enough, then everything would

be all right. But was I living by faith or by wishful thinking?

Jesus never encouraged his friends to cover over the pain

in their lives, but to bring it into the light,

where healing is found.

9

F A I T H

God has promised to complete the work he began in me.

He may not do that in ways that make sense to me, but I have

his promise that what he began, he will finish.

All I have to do is to take the next step.

The path may not look familiar, but it's the road home.

F A I T H

Like an addict who craves a bigger and better high,

the believer often craves more intense religious feelings.

When we live our lives as if God exists for us—

to make us happy—we have missed the point completely.

What does that self-indulgent euphoria have to do

with Calvary?

F A I T H

We place so much emphasis on success and achievement,

on accomplishment and numbers.

But God is singularly unimpressed with all the

paraphernalia we have attached to our faith.

What God cares about is who I am when the lights are off.

F A I T H

I believe that God would have us live

trusting him at every turn.

It was hard for me to let go, to truly trust Christ

for my every breath, but as I continue on this journey now,

I know as deep as the marrow in my bones

there is no other way to live.

F A I T H

I know that my Redeemer lives;

What joy that blest assurance gives!

He lives, he lives who once was dead;

He lives, my everlasting head.

. . . .

He lives to bless me with his love,

And still he pleads for me above;

He lives to raise me from the grave,

And me eternally to save.

—*SAMUEL MEDLEY*

F A I T H

A mountain of faith isn't going to move a mustard seed.

It all depends on what your faith is in. Having more faith

in a misconceived God doesn't work.

And we have come to have faith in faith,

rather than faith in God.

F A I T H

I don't always understand what the Lord is doing

in and through my life. And yet God in his faithfulness

holds on to us when we "don't like the plan."

God still loves, still goes after, still stands true and faithful.

Even if we are faithless, he promises

to remain faithful (2 Timothy 2:13).

F A I T H

There's a story told about Michelangelo

walking down the street, pushing a very large rock.

Some passerby asked him why he was taking such pains

with an old rock. The artist's answer?

"There's an angel in this rock that wants to come out."

What dream has God buried in you?

What does the angel in your rock look like?

As Christians, whatever our specific ministry might be,

we are called to a "ministry of reconciliation"

as "Christ's ambassadors" (2 Corinthians 5:17–21).

We're not representing ourselves or our own agenda;

we're representing Christ.

F A I T H

What I used to know in my head,

I now know in my heart.

It is one thing to believe in the ability of a surgeon

to perform life or death surgery on your body;

it is quite another to allow yourself to be put to sleep

and submit yourself to his knife.

19

F A I T H

O LORD, you are my God; I will exalt you

and praise your name, for in perfect faithfulness

you have done marvelous things,

things planned long ago.

ISAIAH 25:1

20

F A I T H

If you live on a pedestal, you spend half your time

watching that you don't fall off. But as you walk in the truth

of who you are in Christ you are empowered to "let go and let God."

The truth is that God matters and we matter to him,

and that's about it.

F A I T H

Matthew 10:39 says: "Whoever finds his life will lose it,

and whoever loses his life for my sake will find it."

Finding one's life is possible—but only by finding it in him

and only by throwing off our reliance on the extras.

Let us keep our eyes on Jesus,

not on what others will think of us.

F   A   I   T   H

One writer has said that there is a crack in everything

God has made. This is not, however, a license to live

in a careless way in hopes that our subsequent brokenness

will teach us more about the grace and mercy of God.

As Paul said, "Shall we go on sinning so that grace may increase?

By no means!" (Romans 6:1-2).

F A I T H

When greatness seems to vanish

Faster than the morning mist—

. . . .

I stand alone, I'm smiling in the dark.

He who would be greatest must be the servant of all.

I hear it now, a softer, truer call.

F A I T H

A softer call, "Come to me, all you who are weary and burdened,

and I will give you rest" (Matthew 11:28).

A truer call, "What does the LORD require of you?

To act justly and to love mercy and to walk humbly

with your God" (Micah 6:8).

I hear it now.

F A I T H

For some it is a slow process of coming to faith;

for others it is a sudden confrontation on the road.

But for all of us, when we are called from death to life,

when we discover what we were really made for,

heaven celebrates our birth.

F A I T H

Satan is not out for our best interests.

He rejoices in our defeats, in our discouragement.

He rejoices when he gets us to believe the lies.

But he does not have the last word.

Romans 8 starts with a wonderful line:

"Therefore there is now no condemnation for those

who are in Christ Jesus."

No condemnation.

F A I T H

Called to love with hearts as strong and deep as rivers run,

Called to live beyond ourselves, beyond the webs we've spun,

Called to laugh with those who laugh, to cry, to weep, to sing,

to give ourselves, to live an offering.

F A I T H

Our impatience to have God move now will drive us to
take control of our lives. We can choose to bow the knee now
and ask him to forgive us for trying to squeeze the answer we want
out of heaven, or we will bow the knee later in remorse
thinking that we knew better than God.

F A I T H

We imagine that if good things happen, then God loves us

and if life seems difficult, then he doesn't.

This isn't true.

Join hands with God in your life. Throw open the doors and let

the sun come pouring in. God is talking to us all the time.

God is at work!

F A I T H

On the next sunny day go out and take a look at how closely your shadow follows you. It doesn't have an opinion of its own. It doesn't have its own agenda. Wherever you go it follows you. This is a picture of the life secure in Christ. Nothing to prove, nothing to hide, and nothing to fear.

F A I T H

There is rest to be found in surrendering our quest for significance
to God, accepting that we have no worth apart from Christ.
The God of the universe values your life so much
that he gave his Son to die in your place. That should bring us
to our knees and give dignity to our souls.

F   A   I   T   H

I choose to live with intentionality, aware of my weakness

apart from Christ but bringing it to him constantly.

Try it: Give him your weakness and let him prove his strength.

Paul tried it: "For Christ's sake, I delight in weaknesses …

For when I am weak, then I am strong" (2 Corinthians 12:10)

—in Christ.

F A I T H

From when the sun begins to rise,

Golden rays across the skies,

I will kneel at your feet,

Here I'll fall . . .

After all I will be found in you;

After all you are the only truth.

After all I will be found in you, word of wisdom;

For the only way I'll stand straight and tall

Is to find my life in you, after all.

— *SHEILA WALSH*

F A I T H

Often we cling more to our theory of who God is
than to who he really is as he has revealed himself in Christ
and through his Word.
Books too often take the place of God's Word.
We ingest the opinions and experiences of men or women
who no doubt love the Lord, but whose words should never
take the place of scriptural revelation.

F A I T H

Sometimes God does not seem to be faithful,

because he doesn't answer our prayers as we expected him to.

If I will bring every jagged edge of my life to him,

he will continue to mold me to become the woman I am called to be.

Whatever is happening with you right now, meditate on these words:

GOD IS FAITHFUL.

F A I T H

We are called to walk by faith.

We hold on to the promises of God not because they seem likely,

for at times they don't,

but because they come from God

and it is not possible for him to lie.

F A I T H

In our desire to be an inspiration to one another we often

veil what is true, because what is true is not always inspirational.

But hurting believers whose lives are in tatters often need real help.

If we were able to put aside our need for approval long enough to

be authentic, then, surely, we would be living as the church.

F A I T H

As I pull my mind and heart away from myself and tune in

to the greatness and goodness of God, my faith is matured.

He never holds himself back from us.

When we give ourselves to him, we present worship with flesh on it,

a gift with content, words undergirded by our lives.

F A I T H

When we get away from the invasive noise and activity

of this world, when we tune into our relationship with Christ,

we discover the wonder that we are waiting for.

We can wait for wonder to come knocking at our door.

But if we will be quiet and listen,

we will hear it knocking at our hearts.

F A I T H

I see my soul as being like my car.

As a vehicle needs clean oil, I need intimate contact with God.

Our souls were made for this. When we deprive our souls

of that very life force, we can survive—

but that is all we are doing.

We were not created to merely survive

but to thrive in God.

F A I T H

I would imagine that in your circle of friends or acquaintances

there are many who feel isolated, who long to live an honest,

transparent life before others and before God.

If you have "been through the valley," perhaps God has

anointed you to reach out and ask others around you

to face the important questions of life.

F A I T H

We Christians have become lazy.

We would rather listen to someone else's interpretation

of the Word of God than read it for ourselves.

And yet, I want to know the things that make him happy

and the things that break his heart.

How can I do that if I don't study his words to me?

F A I T H

It would make so much of the journey more bearable

if we could see that the path that is painful for a time

is leading somewhere and that it will get better.

We don't have that.

No believer who has gone before us has had that.

There is no map; Christ is the Way.

F A I T H

Each one of us has a calling, a place to fill that no one else can.

God does not squeeze us all into lookalike molds;

he doesn't insist that we all care about the same things.

Each one of us has a divine destiny.

When we discover that, we don't minister only to the world,

we minister to the Lord.

F A I T H

Our human flesh cries out for comfort and direction,

and yet we are called to live above that.

Our lives are a journey of faith.

Surely, it is on the path with Christ that we will find rest.

When we are there, we will no longer wonder about

God's will for our lives—we will be living it.

F A I T H

Adam and Eve traded the perfect peace of the Garden

and the deepest, intimate fellowship with God

to grasp for a chance to be like him.

It's only when we lose ourselves in God

that we find a sense of purpose.

F A I T H

It's a mystery to me—this collaboration between the triune God

and his children. But one thing I do know is this:

I can choose to wear myself into the ground trying to produce

something impressive in my life,

or I can rest safe in the arms of Jesus.

F A I T H

Beyond the choices that we make for our lives,

there is a common bond. It is the deepest aspect of ourselves,

the spiritual part that cries out for heaven, that is made

to be a dwelling place for God. Nothing and no one else

can answer that thirst. It is the size of eternity.

F A I T H

I prayed a very simple but life-changing prayer:

"Father, I stand before you now with empty hands.

Whatever you put in my hands, I will welcome

and whatever you take away, I will gladly let it go."

The prayer was relatively easy.

Walking it out daily is what would prove difficult.

F A I T H

When I fail, I am grateful for the mercy and forgiveness of God.

Because I am so strong willed, it is important for me to surrender

to God without a barrage of questions—

to *choose* to obey as an act of will.

F A I T H

Whatever you are carrying, take it to Jesus.

That may sound simple and trite, but it is the very best choice

that any of us can make.

He who knelt in the garden and wept tears of blood

understands the agony that tears at your soul.

HOPE

H O P E

"'For I know the plans I have for you,' declares the LORD,

'plans to prosper you and not to harm you,

plans to give you hope and a future.'"

JEREMIAH 29:11

H O P E

I never knew you lived so close to the floor,

but every time I am bowed down,

crushed by this weight of grief,

I feel your hand on my head, your breath on my cheek,

your tears on my neck.

You never tell me to pull myself together,

to stem the flow of many tears.

You simply stay by my side for as long as it takes,

so close to the floor.

H O P E

I wonder sometimes if we think it ungodly to mourn

the changing seasons of life, as if doing so were to question

God's wisdom. Everything in our lives comes to us

through the gracious hands of the Lord,

but that does not mean our lives will be free of pain.

H O P E

The first step in dealing with our disappointments

is to admit them and admit that we are powerless to change them.

Admit you are needy, wounded by the past, hurt and confused

by the present. It is only when we confess these things to God

that he can fill the broken, empty places with his joy.

H O P E

Running to hide our faces in God is not like seeking the comfort

and familiarity of a childhood blanket

that allows us to tune out the realities of our lives.

God is a mighty lion, whose roar is heard in every corner of the world.

Still, when you are in trouble, you can run to him.

There you will find strength to live your life.

H O P E

There is an ache within my soul,

A longing deep as rivers roll,

An ancient song, a song of praise,

To hear your voice and see your face . . .

And I shall walk upon this earth

Until my journey finds its end;

Then I shall stand by amazing grace,

And hear your voice and see your face.

— SHEILA WALSH

H O P E

Winter is a cold, harsh season that offers little comfort or shelter.

It is a bleak and weary landscape, but underneath that heavy blanket,

there is life, new life; it just takes time.

As I understand God's Word, it is not the pace of the race that matters,

but that we all finish together.

H O P E

God will lovingly push us inch by inch to chip away

the hard edges of our lives, to refine us into a work of art

in which others will see his hand. Though such refining is never easy,

it is what we were created for. Too often we settle for a mere existence

when the hope of life is waiting inside the rock.

H O P E

The LORD is my light and my salvation—whom shall I fear?

The LORD is the stronghold of my life—of whom shall I be afraid?

PSALM 27:1

H O P E

David had been a shepherd boy. From time to time lions or bears
would try to carry a lamb away, but David was right there,
slingshot in hand, ready to fight for the lamb's life.
If David had run away as a boy, he would have run away as an adult;
instead, he grabbed hold of his fear and reined it in.

H O P E

There is so much more to life than mere survival!

God wants you to live, not just get through one more day.

We can try in vain to fix ourselves, but only the One who made us

knows the path to healing.

H O P E

When I felt my life starting to shake, I looked for some *experience*

that would deliver me from my trouble.

I crammed my mind with books and tapes in a frantic search

of a touch from heaven. I never thought to stop all my *doing*

and just listen.

H O P E

There were days I know, not long ago,

When it seemed like the sun would never shine.

There were nights so blue, when I longed for you

To take this fragile life of mine.

But now I'm standing with my face in the Son;

And these are the best days of my life.

— *S H E I L A   W A L S H*

H O P E

It does not matter what brought you to your knees,

what matters is that you are there. I believe that the way home

for all pilgrims is through this bitter wasteland.

It is there when all help and all hope is gone, that we finally learn

to trust in the only One who can teach us how to live.

H O P E

We arrive at this rusted, uninviting gateway [of suffering]

through many different circumstances—some out of our control

and some that we have brought upon ourselves.

But if our trust is in Christ, he will pilot us through the deepest valleys

and we will never be the same again.

H   O   P   E

Do you ever despair when it seems the finish line is a long way off

and you're tired out already?

There is joy and comfort to be found in this promise:

"He who began a good work in you will carry it on to completion

until the day of Christ Jesus" (Philippians 1:6).

We are called, but God will do it.

H   O   P   E

In seeking my security and strength in the approval of others,

I would rise or fall at their dictate.

Fear was making it easy for me to be controlled by people,

but I must be controlled only by Christ.

H O P E

There is something you bring with you, when you step out

of the shadows, that no one else can bring.

I know it is hard to change, but it is not too late;

you just have to seize the moment and begin.

You are not alone. Christ will be with you

every step of the way.

71

H O P E

It is dark, Lord.

I feel so alone . . .

I know that you are with me;

chart me through this long, dark night. Amen.

It takes time to hear God in the darkness. It will take quiet, and "in

quietness and trust is your strength" (Isaiah 30:15).

H O P E

When you find yourself in a bleak place,

it is time to pay attention to what God would say to you

in the darkness.

You might be surprised by what he will show you about your life.

I know I was.

H O P E

A woman was obviously very distressed.

What could I say to her? I simply listened and cried with her

and told her how sorry I was. She had needed a chance to speak,

to be heard, to cry out, to beat her hands against the wall,

to have someone hold onto her in the midst of her pain . . .

H O P E

We all need to hear beyond what is said to what remains unsaid

just under the surface.

If we will learn to reach out to and hold on to each other

through the maelstrom of words,

we will find companionship on our journey

that makes the dark days that much more bearable.

H O P E

We sat there for a while holding hands,

tears pouring down our cheeks.

There was nothing to say; nothing that would make it any better.

I didn't come up with any clever words or magic prayers.

We just sat for a while together, two people who love God,

sharing the heartbreak of life and death.

We touched for a moment and left

knowing our only hope is the Lord.

H O P E

When you step out from the shadows into the storm,

you may be at the mercy of the wind for a while,

but Christ is Lord over the wind and the storms,

and you will be truly alive—

not just a whisper of who God called you to be.

H O P E

Perhaps it seems to you that you are at the breaking point.

I urge you in the name of the Lord to throw yourself on him,

to hide yourself under his wings. Don't give up. The road ahead

may look bleak, but trust in God. It is the way home.

H O P E

As long as I viewed someone as the enemy,

I gave that person some power over my life.

But as I forgave a person, I too was free.

I could thank God for his never-ending grace and forgiveness

and get on with the rest of my life.

H   O   P   E

Give your pain to God. Let go of it!

We can become so defined by our trauma

that we feel naked without it.

God will give you a new suit of clothes to wear—

"the oil of gladness instead of mourning,

and a garment of praise

instead of a spirit of despair" (Isaiah 61:3).

H O P E

We know from the story of Job that at times God will allow our lives to be disrupted. [Yet] God is passionately committed to the kind of woman that I *become,* not to what I *do.*

H O P E

I feel your presence here;

I know that you are near.

My soul is thirsty for your loving touch.

My heart cries out to you,

I long for more of you;

Have mercy on me for I need your love ...

H O P E

And I hear your voice on the wind,

And I see your face all around,

And I feel your touch in my soul,

And hope is real to me.

— *SHEILA WALSH & STACY FRENES*

H O P E

Many of us carry around a heavy weight of discouragement.

It seems as if nothing will ever get any better, nothing will change.

In the midst of that I offer these words of hope, of promise—

"God is faithful; he will not let you be tempted

beyond what you can bear" (1 Corinthians 10:13).

H O P E

There is a time for everything …

a time to be born and a time to die,

a time to plant and a time to uproot,

a time to kill and a time to heal,

a time to tear down and a time to build,

a time to weep and a time to laugh,

a time to mourn and a time to dance.

ECCLESIASTES 3:1 – 4

85

H O P E

If we do not tear down, we can never lastingly build.

If we do not take time to mourn, we will have no joy in dancing,

and if we do not fall down on our faces at times and weep,

we will never be swept away with laughter.

H O P E

Dear Lord,

You are full of surprises.

From the darkest night

comes the most breathtaking sunrise.

From the most unforgiving rain

comes the sweetest refreshment.

Thank you for unexpected gifts.

Amen.

H O P E

Looking at things in the light has a way of reducing many of them
to an appropriate size. Unspoken fears can take on
terrifying dimensions, but when brought into the open with God,
his perfect love casts out our fear.

H O P E

Think of the story of Joseph.

When he finally revealed to his brothers that he—the governor

of Egypt—was the kid brother they had sold into slavery,

they feared for their lives. Joseph told them not to be afraid;

what they had intended for evil, God meant for good.

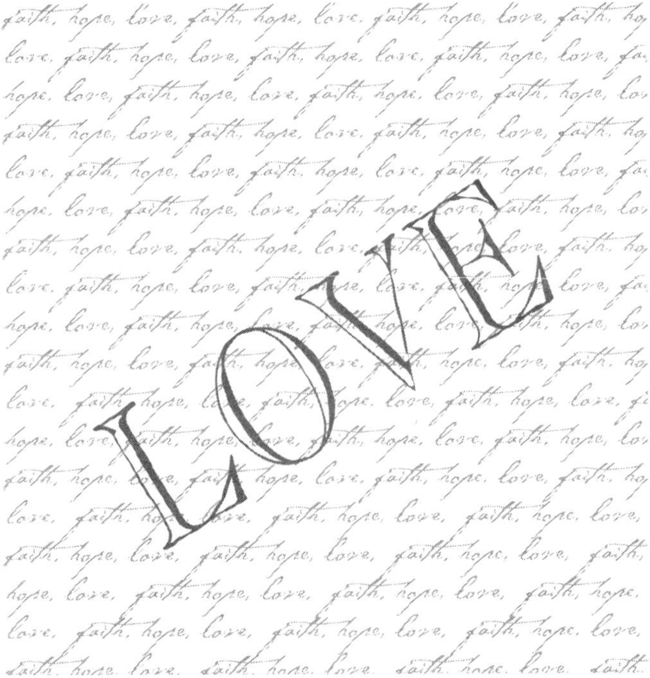
LOVE

L O V E

Jesus said: "A new command I give you: Love one another.

As I have loved you, so you must love one another."

JOHN 13:34

L O V E

Only the grace of God can open our eyes so that we are spiritually

clear-sighted. Christ has a heart for healing blind people.

Underneath the healing flow

miracles of mercy grow.

Sight is given to the blind

washed again a second time.

Wash me now, dear Lord.

L O V E

When I gave up and gave myself to God,

when I told him how helpless and hopeless I was,

God didn't cover or excuse a thing.

He didn't disagree with me on one point,

but in my surrender he assured me that he loved me.

L O V E

Here is love vast as the ocean—

Loving kindness as the flood,

When the Prince of life our ransom

Shed for us his precious blood.

Who his love will not remember?

Who can cease to sing his praise?

He can never be forgotten,

Throughout heaven's eternal days.

L O V E

Self-absorption makes some of us feel as if we have nothing
to offer to the Christian family, so we retreat to a spiritual bed-rest
and do nothing. Our self-absorption destroys our relationships
with other people; it makes us incapable of loving others.

L O V E

My natural instinct is to stay away from what might be painful,

to write people off and move on,

but that is never the way of the Cross.

I lived that way for too long, and it is the way of the coward.

I want to deal with life honestly, seeking restoration

wherever possible.

96

L O V E

We are called to bless God with our lives.

We think that God is there to bless us; we think there should be

some benefit to us at every moment.

God does not exist just to make our lives better;

we exist so that we can learn to love and worship him

in spirit and in truth.

L O V E

Part of being fully alive to God is being willing

to embrace all that he puts in our path,

so that we can become more like him.

When I study the life of Christ, I sense a deep, rich symphony

ascending to the heart of God—using every note and inflection.

This is what we, too, were made for.

L O V E

Jesus' twofold commandment to love God and others as ourselves

calls for a depth of love that I do not yet know.

But there is a strong candle burning.

Vital life lessons are learned in community as we are forced

to face ourselves as we really are

and love enough to want to change.

L O V E

We can all begin to change how we live.

We can be more real and present in our families.

We can take our eyes off ourselves and our own journey

and realize that this is a group outing—that we are not supposed to

arrive in heaven alone but hand in hand.

L O V E

You love me Lord, teach me to love.

You fill me Lord, teach me to give.

You are my joy, my heart, my vision.

You are my life, sweet breath of heaven.

Pour through me celestial leaven.

Bread for the hungry, life for the living.

L O V E

Jesus says—if you love me, feed my sheep.

This assumes that God will give us something to feed them with—

not that we will have to "create the food" ourselves.

As we abide in the true vine, the true vine is also the Bread of Life—

and there's enough to go around.

L O V E

I was what I call a "quiet terrorist," someone who liked to

quietly control things from the sidelines.

I now value genuine feedback from close friends very highly.

It takes courage to confront one another in love.

When I harbor feelings in my heart that I don't lovingly tell

the other person about, then I am controlling the situation

rather than giving that person a chance.

L O V E

Friends who confront us with our weaknesses but never
build us up are like "Job's comforters" who tear at us piece by piece.
We all need to hear encouragement. We need our strengths to be
named and appreciated. We need to love each other so actively
that we speak both words of challenge and words of hope.

L O V E

There are seasons in all of our lives when the wind blows cold and we feel fragile and exposed. These are the times when we wrap each other up in a blanket of love and friendship and stay right there until the buds begin to show again.

L O V E

Dear Father, who forgives all our sins,

who showers us with mercy and compassion,

teach us to love as you love;

teach us to forgive as you forgive;

teach us to live as you lived.

For Christ's sake, Amen.

L O V E

God loves you.

He looks at you with your list of the things that disqualify you,

tears up your list, and places a kiss on both cheeks.

Turn your eyes upon Jesus. Receive the love he freely offers.

See yourself as God's beloved.

L O V E

Stop for a moment and take a look at yourself in the mirror.

Allow this truth to wash over your face:

God loves me with all of heaven right now,

just as I am: gray hairs, smeared mascara, telltale lines, and all ...

L O V E

Then take a peek inside and allow this truth to wash through
your heart: God loves me just the way I am—quick tempered,
procrastinating, envious or gossipy.
I pray that a year from now I will be a more godly woman
than I am today, but God will not love me one bit more
than he does right at this minute.

L O V E

Satisfy us in the morning with your unfailing love,

that we may sing for joy and be glad all our days.

PSALM 90:14

L   O   V   E

Consider the woman who broke her jar of expensive perfume
over the feet of Jesus. Even though she was criticized by others
for the recklessness of her act, Christ reprimanded her critics,
telling them they did not understand what she had done.
There is no better moment to pour your love out on another.

Carpe diem: Seize the day!

L O V E

God's purposes are for our good, never for our destruction.

We have the comfort of knowing that "He will not let you be tempted

beyond what you can bear" (1 Corinthians 10:13).

This is a concrete promise. At the right time God will say,

"It is enough." Our God is good.

L O V E

Our world is littered with broken, bitter people who need love.

By love, I do not mean a soft, quiet thing, but a powerful force for good.

Love breaks down and builds up. It is transforming.

L O V E

Everywhere I went, I found "real people."

In my days of trying to be perfect, life had been all about me.

Now I realized that my life was supposed to be about others.

Now I was "real" too.

L O V E

On the mount of crucifixion

Fountains opened deep and wide,

Through the floodgates of God's mercy

Flowed a vast and gracious tide.

Grace and love like mighty rivers

Poured incessant from above;

And heaven's peace and perfect justice

Kissed a guilty world in love.

— TRADITIONAL

L O V E

God in his mercy, out of a desire for a real relationship with us,

will continue to allow us to fall flat on our faces until all we want

is him. He is so committed to our spiritual health and growth

that he will do whatever it takes to free us

from our selfish nature.

He knows us well and loves us lavishly.

L O V E

Relationships are the only things

that have eternity written all over them.

We need to "find ourselves" in Christ and in relationship

with one another. It is in relationship that we see our strengths

and our weaknesses and find the courage to change.

L O V E

The nameless woman whom Jesus met at the well

was scarred and bruised, but her wounds were in her spirit.

Not until she came face-to-face with Christ

did she catch a glimpse of what she was really made for.

When Jesus confronted her with who she was

and then offered her a better way to live,

she grasped hold of it with every fiber of her being.

L O V E

What a gift Christ gave her.

He loved her enough to let her know,

"I know it all, and I still love you."

That unfamiliar and glorious gift changed her life so that,

even as she was gulping it down,

she was running to tell others the Good News.

L O V E

"I know it all, and I still love you."

That is the convicting, convincing, liberating truth

that comes from an encounter with Christ.

I imagine the Samaritan was a changed woman after that day.

After encountering Jesus, she was fully known and fully loved

for the first time in her life.

She had looked into the face of God, and he was smiling.

L O V E

Gracious Father,

You know us so well.

You love us so completely.

Forgive us, we pray,

for hiding in the shadows.

Give us the courage to live in the light,

for you are Light,

and you are Truth,

and we are your children. Amen.

L O V E

It is clear that we are to hold one another accountable

for our lives, but when discipline is necessary

we are to do it with tears in our eyes.

Because not one of us knows what tomorrow will bring,

let us sow mercy in the lives of others,

so that God will be merciful to us.

L O V E

God loves me because that is who he is.

There is nothing I can do to make it happen.

It already has.

Without God, without what Jesus has already done for me,

I'm not lovable at all, but because of him I am loved

with a love that will last forever.

It's a gift. Pure gift!

L   O   V   E

The Lord's love is a strong love that does not flatter

or overlook our sinful nature:

"For he knows how we are formed,

he remembers that we are dust" (Psalm 103:14).

L O V E

When you carefully guard your image,

you don't take risks to reach out to others;

you dispense your time and love in tiny portions.

Jesus was never like that. He lavished himself on the great strugglers

of the world, those who wrestled and failed with their humanity.

He talked to them; he listened and lovingly spoke

the undiluted truth.

L O V E

You alone are the Savior of my heart,

Faithful in all you do.

You alone are the keeper of my soul,

Tender and kind and true.

I will seek you in the morning.

I will seek your face at night.

How lovely is your presence to me, O Lord to me.

— SHEILA WALSH

L O V E

I begin each day with a prayer of thanks that I am living

in the midst of God's abundant, full life. I have good friends

who love me and whom I love. When the Lord brings to my mind

something I need to "deal with," I make a commitment to do so

at the first possible moment. My life feels light.

L O V E

"Surely goodness and love will follow me all the days of my life,

and I will dwell in the house of the LORD forever" (Psalm 23:6).

What a promise!